ALTERNATOR BOOKS™

WHO INVENTED THE
RADIO?

TESLA VS. MARCONI

Susan E. Hamen

Lerner Publications ◆ Minneapolis

For my dad, the ham radio enthusiast, and the childhood kitchen-table memories of listening to astronauts' transmissions from space with him. *CQ.*

Lerner Publications Company
A division of Lerner Publishing Group, Inc.
241 First Avenue North
Minneapolis, MN 55401 USA

For reading levels and more information, look up this title at www.lernerbooks.com.

Main body text set in Aptifer Slab Regular 11.5/18.
Typeface provided by Linotype AG.

Library of Congress Cataloging-in-Publication Data
Names: Hamen, Susan E., author.
Title: Who invented the radio? : Tesla vs. Marconi / Susan E. Hamen.
Description: Minneapolis : Lerner Publications, 2018. | Series: STEM smackdown | Includes bibliographical references and index. | Audience: Ages 8–12. | Audience: Grades 4 to 6.
Identifiers: LCCN 2017022029 (print) | LCCN 2017024191 (ebook) | ISBN 9781512483277 (eb pdf) | ISBN 9781512483208 (lb : alk. paper) | ISBN 9781541512092 (pb : alk. paper)
Subjects: LCSH: Radio—History—Juvenile literature. | Tesla, Nikola, 1856–1943—Juvenile literature. | Marconi, Guglielmo, 1874–1937—Juvenile literature. | Inventions—Juvenile literature.
Classification: LCC TK6550.7 (ebook) | LCC TK6550.7 .H36 2018 (print) | DDC 621.384092/2—dc23
LC record available at https://lccn.loc.gov/2017022029

Manufactured in the United States of America
1-43333-33153-9/5/2017

CONTENTS

TUNE IN!

A song plays softly from the speakers of a car speeding down the highway. The driver clicks off the radio, but the radio waves broadcasting the song are still present, invisible in the night air.

In a nearby building, two scientists are harvesting, or collecting, radio waves that are not being used. The scientists have discovered that the energy from unused radio waves can power small devices such as smoke alarms. Instead of letting this energy go to waste, they work to turn these radio waves into usable power. Just like all-star inventors years before them, these scientists are investigating the potential of radio waves. This exciting modern work could be just as important as the invention of the first radio.

Radio technology has come a long way since this early 1914 radio model.

The future of radio technology might mean harnessing unused radio waves as a source of energy.

The radio allows humans to harness radio waves to **transmit** sound. The invention of the radio revolutionized communication in the early twentieth century, replacing telegraph systems, which delivered information by sending electric signals through long-distance wires. Since radio transmissions came through the air instead of along telegraph wires, radios could be used just about anywhere. The new technology completely reshaped society. Suddenly, millions of listeners could tune in to hear news, music, entertainment, and advertisements. An entire industry was born!

But competition to invent the radio was fierce. Two inventors squared off in a race to be the champion of the radio. Who came out on top? Many people say Guglielmo Marconi is the winner in the battle to invent the radio. Others claim that a challenger, Nikola Tesla, holds the title. Tune in to the play-by-play action to see who really deserves credit for this incredible invention.

CHAPTER 1
THE DEFENDING CHAMP

In 1884 a young scientist named Nikola Tesla left his job in Europe and came to the United States. The rookie found a job assisting inventor and businessman Thomas Edison on his work with electricity. But before long, the brilliant young Tesla struck out on his own.

In his New York **laboratory**, Tesla began investigating ways to make wireless lighting possible. He made his first big solo play when he invented the Tesla coil in 1891. The device harnessed and converted electricity into a form that would leave the coil in an electrical arc. It was a slam-dunk invention. Tesla had created technology that would transmit electricity without any wires. This groundbreaking new invention sparked Tesla's curiosity about the possibility of wireless communication.

The Tesla coil (*above*) is made up of two open circuit coils connected by a spark gap—a space where electricity travels between the two coils.

ASSIST

A German physicist named Heinrich Hertz became the first person to send and receive radio waves (*right*). Beginning in 1885, he conducted experiments in his laboratory in Karlsruhe, Germany. Hertz was able to produce electromagnetic waves. These waves can travel through space without being transported by a physical substance, such as metal or a wire. Electromagnetic waves traveling at the right frequency are radio waves. The electromagnetic radio waves, later called Hertzian waves, became a key development and were used by future radio inventors.

GETTING IN THE GAME

Scientists including Heinrich Hertz and David Hughes had started working on radio technology, but they hadn't managed to develop a practical, usable system. Tesla believed his Tesla coil might work for radio power too. In 1893 he set up an experiment to test his new device. Sending a signal through an **antenna** and large city water pipes, Tesla walked around the city with a **receiver** in a wooden box to test his

invention. He put the box on the ground in places all around the city and listened for a signal through the receiver. He could detect sounds more than a mile (1.6 km) from his laboratory!

Tesla loved to discover new things. In this photo, he tried to electrically charge his body by using a coil responsive to the waves transmitted by one of his inventions.

HE DID WHAT?

Tesla (*left*) was an extremely hard and often unconventional worker. He claimed to need only two hours of sleep a night and seemed to work around the clock. While testing his inventions, he was very particular about his surroundings. Tesla was obsessed with cleanliness and easily annoyed by unusual things. For instance, he could not stand the sight of pearls. If his secretary wore them, Tesla would send her home.

Tesla realized he could transmit and receive powerful radio signals if his transmitter and receiver were tuned to the same frequency. That same year, Tesla invented the **oscillator**, which used a steam engine to produce a strong electric current. Could it help him perfect the first basic radio? He was certainly taking the lead in this race.

But Tesla hadn't planned on an opponent who lived thousands of miles away.

CHAPTER 2

THE CHALLENGER

Tesla gave public demonstrations of his Tesla coil, and soon after, word spread about the "mad scientist" who was working on wireless communication. But he was not the only player in the radio game. Guglielmo Marconi, a young Italian inventor, started experimenting with radio waves in 1894 after reading every scientific journal and article he could find about the topic—including those on Tesla's inventions. He too envisioned creating what Tesla called wireless **telegraphy**.

Even as a young boy, Guglielmo was interested in electrical science and studied the works of scientists, including James Clerk Maxwell, Heinrich Hertz, and Oliver Lodge.

ASSIST

An Englishman named Oliver Lodge (*right*) developed a way to detect Hertzian waves in an electrically charged tube in 1893. The tube, called a coherer, could send an invisible, silent signal produced by Hertzian waves from a transmitter to a receiver. When the signal reached the receiver, the coherer caused a bulb to light up or a bell to ring. It was an early step on the path to radio technology.

PERFECTING THE PLAY

Marconi set to work in a stuffy attic workshop at his father's country estate in Pontecchio, Italy, tinkering with his experiments and reviewing the playbooks of earlier contenders in the battle of the radio. He experimented with Oliver Lodge's coherer. He reduced the size of the coherer's glass tube and created a **vacuum** inside the tube to remove the air. He then used a small lever with a knob at the end called a Morse key to send and stop Hertzian waves through the tiny coherer. With these tests, Marconi managed to invent a transmitter that generated and sent electromagnetic waves carrying signals to a receiver. Marconi was catching up to Tesla.

A reproduction of Marconi's first transmitter with an antenna

SCORE!

With a few more adjustments, Marconi's wireless communication system was working and he even succeeded in sending signals about a mile (1.6 km). Without realizing it, he had just evened the playing field with Tesla. Could Marconi perfect his early radio system before Tesla completed his?

Marconi performed many of his early experiments at his father's house, including this one in his father's garden.

CHAPTER 3
THE GREAT RADIO RACE

Tesla and Marconi seemed to be neck and neck in the race to develop a basic radio. But in 1895, Tesla suffered a devastating setback. Just as he was preparing to test the transmission of a wireless signal from his laboratory to a point 50 miles (80 km) away, a fire destroyed his lab. He lost ten years' worth of work. A newspaper reporter wrote, "The destruction of Nikola Tesla's workshop, with its wonderful contents, is . . . a misfortune to the whole world."

As Tesla worked to bounce back from the staggering blow, Marconi

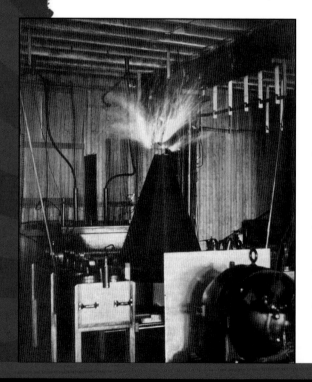

Before the fire of 1895, Tesla's New York laboratory was filled with his inventions and experiments.

Marconi convinced William Preece (*above*) that radio technology would be useful for the post office. This fast new form of communication wouldn't require the current system of telegraph wires.

moved to England. In 1896 he met William Preece, the chief engineer of the post office, and convinced him that his new technology would help post offices send and receive communications. Marconi had found a useful teammate. Preece went to bat for Marconi and recruited offers to help fund Marconi's research.

British post office engineers witnessed some of Marconi's experiments. Here they inspect Marconi's radio equipment during a demonstration in 1897.

With the extra funding, Marconi improved his technology until he could transmit through walls and distances of almost 9 miles (14 km). In 1897 he was granted a **patent** of his wireless system in England. Marconi seemed to be pulling ahead of his competition.

GETTING BACK IN THE GAME

Back in New York, Tesla had recovered enough of his work to apply for a US patent in 1897. He returned to experimenting and made an important discovery that would allow him to send signals even farther. He figured out how he could send messages up to 100 miles (161 km) once he built the technology he needed! But Tesla's breakthrough was matched with a triumphant shot by Marconi.

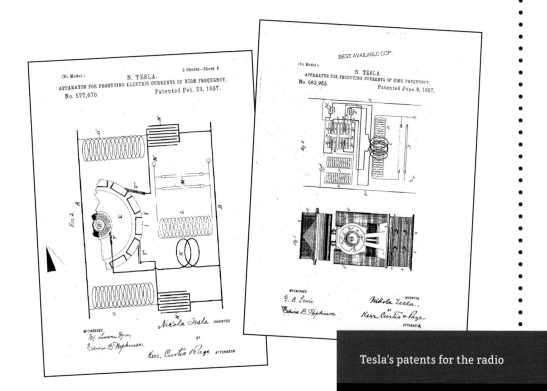

Tesla's patents for the radio

In March 1899, Marconi sent a message across the waters of the English Channel from England to France. However, to get the power he needed to send the signal that distance, Marconi used his rival's oscillator. Tesla's very own invention was helping the competition beat him!

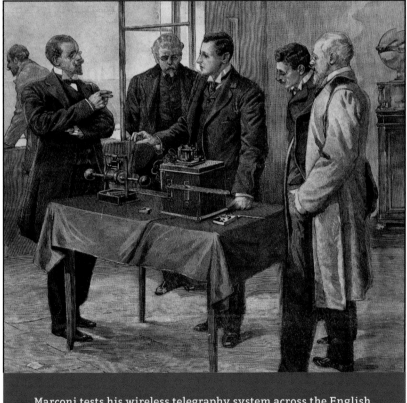

Marconi tests his wireless telegraphy system across the English Channel with a room full of witnesses.

Tesla sits in his Colorado Springs laboratory with his invention that increased the strength of his transmitter.

Tesla needed a new strategy if he was ever going to catch up. He set up an experimental station in Colorado Springs, Colorado, in May 1899. The inventor told a newspaper reporter his plans were to "send a message from Pikes Peak to Paris." He then figured out how to increase the strength of his transmitter, and in 1899, he began building a transmission station that he hoped would be able to send messages around the world.

THEY DID WHAT?

During their experiments with radio transmissions, both Tesla and Marconi claimed to receive signals coming from *very* far away! In 1900 Tesla claimed he heard three signals come through his receiver that he believed were from aliens. Nineteen years later, Marconi told reporters that he had also received radio signals from outer space.

STRAIGHT TO THE FINISH LINE

As Tesla began inching ahead in the race to send a long-distance broadcast, Marconi was hot on his tail. In 1900 Marconi built a transmission station in Cornwall, England, and another in Cape Cod, Massachusetts. He tried to send signals between the two but was unsuccessful. Still, Marconi did not give up on his goal of sending a wireless message across the Atlantic Ocean. He set his sights on a slightly shorter trans-Atlantic broadcast.

With his equipment in place, Marconi set sail for St. John's, Newfoundland, in Canada. He had instructed his assistants in Cornwall to send a message every day between 3:00 p.m. and 6:00 p.m. beginning on December 11.

On December 12, Marconi and his assistants in Newfoundland received the wireless signal. His long-distance radio signal was a success! Marconi had inched past the competition to win radio gold. Newspapers announced the success of his trans-Atlantic radio transmission. Marconi's message had traveled 2,100 miles (3,380 km)!

Marconi was granted a US patent for his radio technology in 1904. He was celebrated as the man who came out on top in the great radio race.

CHAPTER 4
AFTER THE BATTLE

The first radio station began broadcasting for home listeners in 1920. Soon radio stations began to pop up throughout the United States. Families were able to purchase affordable radios to receive the broadcasted radio signals. Radio quickly became a revolutionary form of communication, offering news and entertainment.

Some radios were set up with a speaker to broadcast sound to a large group of people.

This woman listens to a radio broadcast through headphones held to her ears in the 1920s.

It looked as though Marconi was the champion of a slam-dunk invention. At the time of Marconi's victory, Otis Pond, an engineer then working for Tesla, said, "Looks as if Marconi got the jump on you."

Radios became common in American households, and so did Marconi's name.

Following the race of the radio invention, Tesla went on to become a pioneer in the technology of X-rays, lasers, and the electric motor.

Tesla replied, "Marconi is a good fellow. Let him continue. He is using seventeen of my patents."

So is Marconi the father of the radio? Not exactly. He can't take all the credit, especially after what happened decades later. In 1943 the US Supreme Court overturned Marconi's 1904 US patent for wireless telegraphy. Evidence had proven that Tesla had invented the radio years before Marconi's US patent. The gold had been in the wrong hands for years! Tesla wasn't even alive anymore. But he had suddenly become the champion of the radio. Although Marconi had been the first competitor to succeed in long-distance radio transmission, he had used Tesla's inventions. Legally, Tesla was the winner.

Both Tesla and Marconi made important advances in the creation of the radio, and their inventions remain a part of our everyday lives. Although some may still argue about who the true champion is, it is safe to say that the battle of the radio was one great matchup.

Although his patent was eventually taken away, Marconi won the Nobel Prize in Physics in 1909 for his developments with wireless telegraphy. He continued to make breakthroughs in the study of different types of electromagnetic waves.

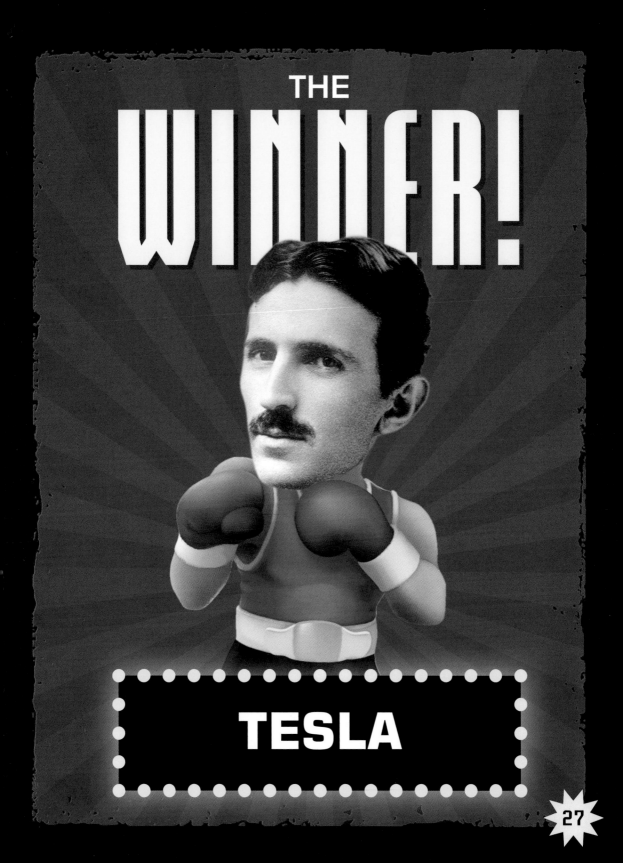

THE **WINNER!**

TESLA

27

INVENTOR MATCHUP

TESLA

- **DEMEANOR:** Energetic showman
- **WORK STYLE:** Many inventions at once
- **NUMBER OF PATENTS:** About 300
- **WINNING MOVE:** Patent holder of wireless telegraphy

VS.

MARCONI

- **DEMEANOR:** Quiet and disciplined
- **WORK STYLE:** Focused on wireless telegraphy
- **NUMBER OF PATENTS:** About 40
- **WINNING MOVE:** First trans-Atlantic radio broadcast

TIMELINE

1891
Nikola Tesla invents the Tesla coil. He files for a patent.

1893
Tesla successfully transmits electromagnetic waves through his transmitter and receives the signal more than a mile (1.6 km) away from his laboratory.

1895
Guglielmo Marconi redesigns the coherer tube and uses it to create his own form of wireless telegraphy.

MARCH 13, 1895
Tesla loses all of his work when his laboratory burns to the ground.

1897
Marconi succeeds in transmitting through walls and up to almost 9 miles (14 km) away. He is granted a British patent for his wireless telegraphy technology. Tesla is granted a US patent.

MARCH 1899
Marconi sends a wireless message across the English Channel.

DECEMBER 11, 1901
Marconi sends and receives a radio signal across the Atlantic Ocean.

1943
The US Supreme Court declares Marconi's patents invalid, citing Tesla's earlier patents for radio.

SOURCE NOTES

14   Marc J. Seifer, *Wizard: The Life and Times of Nikola Tesla: Biography of a Genius* (New York: Citadel, 1998), 146.

19   Ibid., 265.

23   "Who Invented Radio?," *PBS*, accessed May 18, 2017. https://www .pbs.org/tesla/ll/ll_whoradio.html.

25   Ibid.

GLOSSARY

antenna: a metallic wire or rod that sends or receives radio waves

electromagnetic waves: energy waves that have both an electric and magnetic field. Electromagnetic waves can travel without a physical connection between objects.

frequency: the rate of vibration of a sound wave that correlates with radio signals

laboratory: a place that contains special equipment for scientists to use in experiments

oscillator: a device that generates a strong rhythm of electric currents

patent: a legal document that gives an inventor the right to be the only person to make or sell an item. Anyone else must pay the patent holder to use the item.

receiver: a device that converts electromagnetic waves into sound

telegraphy: the use of a telegraph system. A telegraph is an electric device used for sending messages by a code over wires.

transmit: to send a signal by radio waves or over a wire. A radio transmitter transmits radio signals.

vacuum: a space that is sealed and free of air or gases

FURTHER INFORMATION

Guglielmo Marconi
http://www.history.com/topics/inventions/guglielmo
-marconi

How Stuff Works Science: Who Invented the Radio?
http://science.howstuffworks.com/innovation/inventions
/who-invented-the-radio.htm

Kenney, Karen Latchana. *Who Invented the Television: Sarnoff vs. Farnsworth*. Minneapolis: Lerner Publications, 2018.

Marsico, Katie. *Inventor, Engineer, and Physicist Nikola Tesla*. Minneapolis: Lerner Publications, 2018.

Rusch, Elizabeth. *Electrical Wizard: How Nikola Tesla Lit Up the World*. Sommerville, MA: Candlewick, 2013.

A Science Odyssey: Guglielmo Marconi, 1874–1937
http://www.pbs.org/wgbh/aso/databank/entries/btmarc
.html

Smibert, Angie. *12 Great Moments That Changed Radio History*. Mankato, MN: 12-Story Library, 2015.

INDEX

PHOTO ACKNOWLEDGMENTS

The images in this book are used with the permission of: iStock.com/maodesign, p. 1; Wikimedia Commons (CC 1.0 PDM), pp. 4, 7; iStock.com/sureeporn, p. 5; © Museum of Science and Industry, Chicago, USA/Photo © 2014 J.B. Spector/Bridgeman Images, p. 6; Everett Collection/Newscom, p. 8; Roger Viollet/Getty Images, p. 9; Classic Image/Alamy Stock Photo, p. 10; Library of Congress (LC-DIG-ggbain-14387), p. 11; DEA/A. DAGLI ORTI/Getty Images, pp. 12, 18; Science History Images/Alamy Stock Photo, pp. 13, 25; The Granger Collection, New York, p. 14; Science & Society Picture Library/Getty Images, p. 15; Cardiff Council Flat Holm Project/Wikimedia Commons (CC BY 3.0), p. 16; U.S. Patent #577,670, p. 17 (left); U.S. Patent #583,953, p. 17 (right); Wellcome Library, London/Wikimedia Commons (CC BY 4.0), p. 19; NASA/JPL-Caltech/T. Pyle, p. 20; Bettmann/Getty Images, p. 22; Library of Congress (LC-USZ62-23645), p. 23; Library of Congress (LC-DIG-hec-32149), p. 24; Library of Congress (LC-DIG-ggbain-34478), p. 26; Library of Congress (LC-B2-1026-9), pp. 27, 28 (Tesla portrait); Library of Congress (LC-USZ62-39702), p. 28 (Marconi portrait); iStock.com/lushik, p. 28 (boxing glove bullets). Design elements: iStock.com/ivanastar; iStock.com/Allevinatis; iStock.com/subtropica.

Front cover: iStock.com/ivanastar (background); iStock.com/Allevinatis (boxer); Stock.com/maodesign (radio); Library of Congress (LC-USZ62-39702) (Marconi portrait); Library of Congress (LC-B2-1026-9) (Tesla portrait).